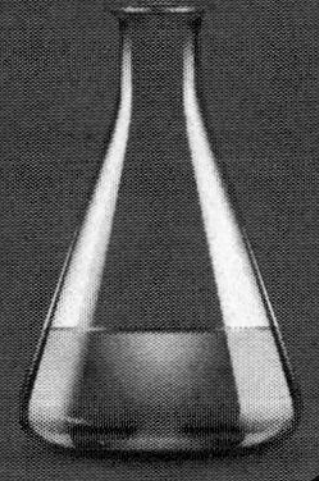

SCIENCE Workbook

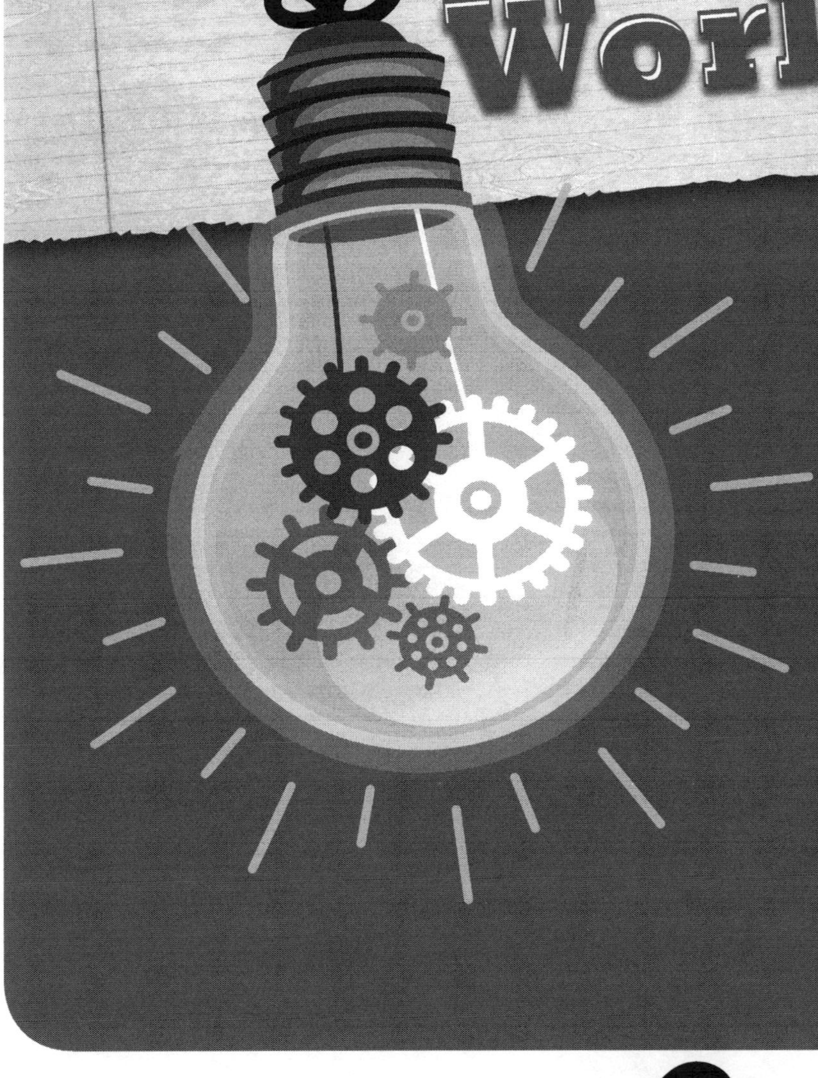

Level 6

Published in Moonstone
by Rupa Publications India Pvt. Ltd 2022
7/16, Ansari Road, Daryaganj
New Delhi 110002

Sales centres:
Allahabad Bengaluru Chennai
Hyderabad Jaipur Kathmandu
Kolkata Mumbai

Copyright © Rupa Publications India Pvt. Ltd 2022

The views and opinions expressed in this book are
the authors' own and the facts are as reported by them
which have been verified to the extent possible,
and the publishers are not in any way liable for the same.

All rights reserved.
No part of this publication may be reproduced, transmitted,
or stored in a retrieval system, in any form or by any means,
electronic, mechanical, photocopying, recording or otherwise,
without the prior permission of the publisher.

ISBN: 978-93-5520-696-1

First impression 2022

10 9 8 7 6 5 4 3 2 1

The moral right of the authors has been asserted.

Printed in India
This book is sold subject to the condition that it shall not,
by way of trade or otherwise, be lent, resold, hired out, or otherwise
circulated, without the publisher's prior consent, in any form of binding
or cover other than that in which it is published.

Contents

Biotic and Abiotic 4

Features of Plants 7

Animal Movements 10

Adapting to Habitat 13

Components of Food 16

Fibre to Fabric 19

Classifying Materials 22

Separation of Substances 26

Changes Around Us 30

Magnets 33

Air and Water 35

Waste Management 38

Light and Reflection 41

Electricity 44

Answers 47

Biotic and Abiotic

1. **Fill in the blanks.**

   a. Plants are also called _____ and autotrophs.

   b. Frogs and lizards are examples of _____ animals.

   c. 70% of the human body consists of _____.

   d. Animals and human beings release _____ during respiration.

   e. The reaction to a stimulus is called a _____.

2. **Write T for true statements and F for false ones.**

   a. Soil and water are important biotic components.

   b. Amoeba is a unicellular organism.

   c. All biotic components are heterotrophs.

   d. All plants are unicellular.

   e. Leaves of a touch me not plant curl up when touched.

3. **Name the following.**

   a. Plants that produce their own food. _____

   b. Animals that feed on dead plants and animals. _____

   c. The uppermost layer of soil. _____

   d. Smallest living structure of a living being. _____

   e. A measure that tells us how hot or cold something is. _____

4. **Short answer questions.**

   a. What are biotic components?
   _____

b. What are abiotic components?

_____

c. What is photosynthesis?

_____

d. Name the abiotic components which affect biotic components.

_____

e. Give two examples of both cold-blooded and warm-blooded animals.

_____

5. Match the following.

Column A	Column B
a. Unicellular organism	Water
b. Autotrophs	Amoeba
c. Decomposer	Vulture
d. Scavenger	Fungi
e. Abiotic	Plants

6. Answer the following questions.

a. Explain the process of respiration.

_____

_____

b. Define stimulus and response. What is the relation between them?

_____

_____

c. Explain the importance of photosynthesis.

_____
_____

d. How are scavengers and decomposers helpful to us?

_____
_____

e. How do the biotic components interact with each other?

_____
_____

7. **Think and write**

   Bacteria, fungi and decomposers help to provide air and nutrients to the soil. How will the fertility of soil be affected in the absence of these? Explain.

   _____
   _____
   _____
   _____

8. **Activity time**

   Collect data from newspapers and other print media about the various factors which disturb the balance of oxygen and carbon dioxide in the atmosphere. Make an action plan to tackle the lack of plants in your neighbourhood and share it in the class.

Features of Plants

1. Fill in the blanks with the correct option.

a. Banana leaves have _____ venation. (reticulate/parallel)

b. Colourful structures surrounding the inner part of a flower are called _____. (petals/sepals)

c. The _____ of a carrot plant store the food. (roots/stem)

d. The desert plants have _____ roots. (shorter/longer)

e. Leaves modify into spines to reduce the loss of _____. (water/air)

2. Write T for true statements and F for false ones.

a. Pollination is important for the growth of new plants.

b. All fruits contain at least one seed.

c. Transpiration takes place through the roots of a plant.

d. Midrib divides the leaf in two parts.

e. Some roots and leaves modify to support the plant.

3. Give two examples of the following.

a. Fruits without seeds. _____, _____

b. Fruits with seeds. _____, _____

c. Plants with modified stem. _____, _____

d. Plants with bulbs. _____, _____

e. Plants with modified roots. _____, _____

f. Plants with tap roots. _____, _____

g. Plants with fibrous roots. _____, _____

4. **Match the following.**

Column A	Column B
a. Ginger	Parallel venation
b. Turnip	Modified leaves
c. Tendrils	Reticulate venation
d. Bamboo leaves	Modified root
e. Mango leaves	Modified stem

5. **Short answer questions.**

   a. What are the different parts of a leaf?

   b. What modifications does the stem undergo to store water?

   c. What is the function of stomata in a plant?

   d. Define the process of transpiration.

   e. What modifications are adopted by Bryophyllum leaves?

6. **Answer the following questions.**

   a. What are the functions of roots? Name different types of roots.

b. What are the functions of the stem in a plant?

_____

_____

c. Explain the process of pollination.

_____

_____

d. Describe how leaf modifications are helpful for plants.

_____

_____

e. What are the functions of a flower in a plant?

_____

_____

7. Think and write

A potato grows under the ground but still it is considered a stem. On the other hand, sweet potato is called a root. Think and write why is it so.

_____

_____

_____

_____

8. Activity time

Draw a colourful diagram of a flower on a chart paper. Label the various parts of the flower.

Animal Movements

1. Fill in the blanks.

a. The joints at the knee and elbow are examples of _____ joint.

b. Birds have a _____ body to help them to fly.

c. Some animals have an outer skeleton called _____.

d. Human bones are filled with _____ which produces blood cells.

e. _____ reduces the friction between the bones.

2. Name two animals which show following movements.

a. Crawl _____, _____

b. Stamp _____, _____

c. Twirl and swim _____, _____

d. Trot _____, _____

e. Climb _____, _____

3. Write the antonyms of the underlined words to form correct sentences.

a. Birds have <u>weak</u> chest muscles.
_____

b. Cockroaches have a hard <u>inner</u> skeleton.
_____

c. Fishes have a <u>rigid</u> backbone.
_____

d. Human body has <u>immovable</u> joints.
_____

e. Animals <u>without</u> a backbone are called vertebrates.
_____

4. Short answer questions.

a. Why is movement important for animals?
_____

b. What are vertebrates? Give examples.
_____

c. What are invertebrates? Give examples.
_____

d. What is cartilage?
_____

e. Name the different types of joints in our body.
_____

5. Answer the following questions.

a. What helps a fish to swim freely in water?
_____
_____

b. What specific features help birds to fly?
_____
_____

c. How do bones and muscles help us to move?
_____
_____

d. What are the functions of human skeleton?

    _____
    _____

e. How does the body of an earthworm help it move?

    _____
    _____

6. Think and write

We can move our legs only to and fro at the knee but in a circular motion at the hip. Explain why is it so?

_____
_____
_____
_____

7. Activity time

X-rays show the exact picture of bones in our body. Collect some old x-rays that are of no use to anyone. Try to look through them and identify various bones and joints.

Adapting to Habitat

1. **Fill in the blanks with the correct option.**

   a. Zebra is commonly found in _____. (rainforests/grasslands)

   b. The _____ uses its hooves and horns to break the ice and find its food. (yak/giraffe)

   c. Stems of _____ plants have air chambers. (aquatic/polar)

   d. Whales have _____ on their heads. (nose/blowholes)

   e. _____ trees shed their leaves once a year. (marine/deciduous)

2. **Write T for true statements and F for false ones.**

   a. A walrus survives in polar region using its long teeth.

   b. Camouflaging helps animals to escape enemies.

   c. Camels have long legs to take long steps in desert.

   d. Rainforest trees have large leaves to prevent sunlight from reaching the surface of the forest.

   e. Ocean and sea are called marine habitats.

3. **Short answer questions.**

   a. Name different types of aquatic habitats.

   _____

   b. Name three types of forest habitats.

   _____

c. How do plants adapt to survive in deserts?

d. How do the plants on the floor of tropical forests survive?

e. How do polar bears survive in the cold habitat?

f. What are the basic adaptations shown by aquatic plants?

g. What helps the ducks to float in water?

4. Name a plant and an animal which lives in the following habitat.

Habitat	Animal	Plant
a. Marine		
b. Freshwater		
c. Temperate Forest		
d. Boreal Forest		
e. Tropical Forest		
f. Grassland		
g. Desert		
h. Mountain		
i. Polar Region		

5. Long answer questions.

a. How do different animals adapt to live in desert?

b. How do dolphins and whales survive in water without gills?

_____

_____

c. Explain how plants and animals manage to survive in grasslands.

_____

_____

d. What is migration? Why do animals migrate?

_____

_____

e. What is camouflage? Name some animals that use this technique.

_____

_____

6. Think and write

Unlike other animals, human beings are known to survive in different types of habitats. Think about it and support the statement with suitable examples.

_____

_____

_____

_____

7. Activity time

Collect pictures of various animals which camouflage. Paste the pictures in your activity file and write the ways in which each animal benefits from it in their life.

Components of Food

1. **Fill in the blanks.**

    a. Carbohydrates give _____ to our body.

    b. Minerals required in small quantities are called _____.

    c. Plants store energy in the form of _____.

    d. Skin diseases are caused due to deficiency of _____.

    e. _____ fats are mostly liquid at room temperature.

2. **Write T for true statements and F for false ones.**

    a. Only children should follow a balanced diet.

    b. Citrus fruits are rich in potassium and vitamin C.

    c. Vitamin A keeps our eyes and hair healthy.

    d. Iron helps in maintaining the water balance.

    e. Calcium regulates the functioning of muscles.

3. **Match the names of diseases to the deficiency of these vitamins or minerals.**

Food Items	Components
a. Goitre	Vitamin C
b. Rickets	Vitamin B
c. Osteoporosis	Iron
d. Beriberi	Vitamin A
e. Scurvy	Vitamin D
f. Anaemia	Calcium
g. Night blindness	Iodine

4. Name two food items which contain the given components.

a. Proteins _____, _____

b. Fats _____, _____

c. Starch _____, _____

d. Sugars _____, _____

e. Roughage _____, _____

5. Short answer questions.

a. Which two types of carbohydrates are present in the food?
   _____

b. What is the other name for roughage?
   _____

c. What are the consequences of deficiency of water in our body?
   _____

d. Name the minerals which are required in large quantities.
   _____

e. How can you make ORS at home?
   _____

6. Answer the following questions.

a. Describe the properties of the two types of fats.
   _____
   _____

b. What is obesity? What are its consequences?
   _____
   _____

c. Describe the effects of protein deficiency.

_____

_____

d. What is a balanced diet? What should be included in it?

_____

_____

e. What are the effects of deficiency of different minerals in our body?

_____

_____

7. **Think and write**

Certain diseases are labelled as deficiency diseases and others are not. How are deficiency diseases different from other diseases? Explain with examples.

_____

_____

_____

_____

8. **Activity time**

Make a food guide pyramid showing the four food groups. Also show the basic food items of each food group that should be included in the diet.

Fibre to Fabric

1. **Fill in the blanks.**

   a. Fibres are woven to make _____.

   b. Cotton and hemp are _____ fibres.

   c. Strands of thread are twisted together to form _____.

   d. Sweaters are made from woollen yarn by _____.

   e. _____ fibre is used as a stuffing in pillows and jackets.

2. **Write T for true statements and F for false ones.**

   a. Khaddar fibre is made by weaving synthetic fibres. ☐

   b. Combing is an important process to extract cotton from the seeds. ☐

   c. Synthetic fibres are obtained from animals. ☐

   d. Coir is obtained from coconut husk. ☐

   e. Jute fibre is obtained from the fruit of jute plant. ☐

3. **Name two objects which can be made using the given fibres.**

   a. Jute _____, _____

   b. Cotton _____, _____

   c. Silk _____, _____

   d. Hemp _____, _____

   e. Flax _____, _____

4. Match the following.

Plant part	Fibre
a. Fruit	Flax
b. Bark	Coir
c. Husk	Kapok
d. Seed	Jute
e. Stem	Cotton

5. Short answer questions.

a. Why do we wear different fabrics in different weather?

b. Name the different types of synthetic fibres.

c. What products can be made using coir?

d. What are synthetic fibres? Name four objects made using them.

e. How is a khaddar cloth different from other cotton clothes?

6. Long answer questions.

a. Why do we need to knit or weave clothes?

b. Describe the steps involved in the production of cotton.

_____

_____

c. Explain the process of retting the jute fibre.

_____

_____

d. Which type of clothes would you wear in winter season? Why?

_____

_____

7. Think and write

The journey of a fibre to become a fabric involves many different machines and tools. Find out and write the names of tools which were used in ancient times as well as those which are used nowadays to make fabric.

_____

_____

_____

_____

8. Activity time

Winter wear is made with different types of woollen fabrics. Find out the animals from which wool is obtained. Collect their pictures and paste them along the collected information in your activity file.

Classifying Materials

1. **Fill in the blanks with the correct option.**

   a. _____ cannot be compressed. (Gasses/Solids)

   b. Wood is an _____ material. (translucent/opaque)

   c. Electric wires are _____ to prevent electric shock. (insulated/heated)

   d. _____ are both magnetic and conductors. (Metals/Gasses)

   e. Particles of _____ are loosely packed. (gases/solids)

2. **Write T for true statements and F for false ones.**

   a. Stones are soluble in kerosene but not in water.

   b. A material can be hard and lustrous both.

   c. Chalk powder can dissolve in water.

   d. All the magnetic materials are insulators also.

   e. Some gases can be dissolved in water.

3. **Complete the table given below by writing Yes or No against each property.**

Material	Lustrous	Float on water	Magnetic	Conductor
a. Wood				
b. Glass				
c. Silver				
d. Rubber				
e. Plastic				

4. Give two examples for the following.

Property	Material 1	Material 2
a. Rough surface		
b. Smooth surface		
c. Translucent		
d. Transparent		
e. Highly lustrous		

5. Short answer questions.

a. Describe the different properties of a pencil.

_____

b. Name four objects which are both hard and rough.

_____

c. Define lustre. Which type of material has this property?

_____

d. What is floatation? Name two objects which show this property.

_____

e. The handles of cooking utensils are made of wood or plastic. Why?

_____

6. **Answer the following questions.**

   a. How are the three states of matter different from each other?

   _____

   _____

   b. What do you understand by miscible and immiscible? How is miscibility different from solubility?

   _____

   _____

   c. Differentiate between conductors and insulators of heat.

   _____

   _____

   d. Electric wires are made using metals and then covered with plastic. Why?

   _____

   _____

   e. How are materials grouped on the basis of their transparency?

   _____

   _____

7. **Think and write**

   Light a torch in a dark room and put your palm over it. Can you see the light of torch through your palm? Conclude whether your palm is opaque, translucent or transparent. Justify your answer.

   _____

   _____

   _____

   _____

8. **Activity time**

   Collect different liquids available in your house like vinegar, lemon juice, honey, oil, milk etc. Mix one spoon of the collected liquids in water and check whether they are miscible or not.

Separation of Substances

1. **Write T for true statements and F for false ones.**

   a. Paper folding is an example of an irreversible change. ☐

   b. Burning of wood is a chemical process. ☐

   c. Tearing of clothes changes the properties of the cloth. ☐

   d. Expansion of liquids can be reversed. ☐

   e. Weathering of rocks is a reversible change. ☐

2. **Categorize the following changes as reversible or irreversible changes.**

   a. Burning a firecracker. _____

   b. A caterpillar changing into butterfly. _____

   c. Blowing a balloon. _____

   d. Evaporation of water. _____

   e. Climbing the stairs. _____

3. **Categorize the following changes as physical or chemical changes.**

   a. Burning of candle wax. _____

   b. Melting of butter. _____

   c. Ripening of mango fruits. _____

   d. Contraction of water in colder region. _____

e. Dissolving salt in a glass of water. _____

4. Rectify the table given below by crossing out the wrong option.

Change	Option 1	Option 2
Burning wood	Permanent	Temporary
Melting of ice cream	Reversible	Irreversible
Breaking of glass	Chemical	Physical
Breaking of a solid glass	Expansion	Contraction
Blooming of flower	Irreversible	Reversible

5. Short answer questions.

a. What is a reversible change?

_____

b. What is an irreversible change?

_____

c. What happens during a chemical change?

_____

d. Why is rusting of iron is an irreversible change?

_____

e. Describe a physical change.

_____

6. **Long answer questions.**

a. What are the different factors which cause changes?

_____

_____

b. Explain why chopping a vegetable is a physical change but cooking it is a chemical change.

_____

_____

c. Give an example of how contraction can be helpful in our daily life.

_____

_____

d. Give two examples of the changes which can be reversed.

_____

_____

e. How does the expansion phenomena work in a thermometer?

_____

_____

7. **Think and write**

   Some physical changes are reversible and some are irreversible. List three of each type in the space given below.

   _____

   _____

   _____

   _____

8. **Activity time**

   Pollution causes many changes in our environment. Make a list of ten such changes and categorize them as permanent or temporary. Identify which of them cause harm to our environment.

Changes Around Us

1. **Choose the correct option for each of the following.**

   a. It is important in the winnowing process

   ☐ Direction of wind ☐ Number of animals

   b. Small pieces of stems or leaves

   ☐ Harvest ☐ Husk

   c. The method to allow the sand to settle down in water

   ☐ Sedimentation ☐ Decantation

   d. Process that can be used to separate stones from rice.

   ☐ Winnowing ☐ Hand-picking

   e. Condensation takes place when water vapours

   ☐ Hit a warm surface ☐ Hit a cool surface

2. **Write T for true statements and F for false ones.**

   a. Filtration process can be used to remove pulp from fruit juices. ☐

   b. Stirring the solution decreases the solubility. ☐

   c. Chalk powder is soluble in water. ☐

   d. Hand-picking is not preferred with a large mixture. ☐

   e. Condensation is same as evaporation. ☐

3. **Describe the following methods of separation.**

   a. Hand-picking _____
   _____

b. Threshing _____

c. Winnowing _____

d. Sieving _____

e. Filtration _____

4. Complete the table given below.

	Solute	Solvent	Solution
a.	Salt		Saline solution
b.		Water	Sugar solution
c.	Chocolate syrup	Milk	
d.		Liquid	Carbonated water
e.	Water vapours	Air	

5. Answer the following questions.

a. Distinguish between a pure substance and a mixture.

b. Under what conditions do we prefer handpicking methods?

c. Explain the process of sedimentation and decantation.

d. What is solubility? How is it related to saturation?

e. Explain the process of obtaining salt from the sea water.

6. Think and write

Different factors such as temperature and motion affect the solubility of a solute in different ways. Identify and write the ways in which solubility can be increased or decreased.

7. Activity time

Observe and identify the ways which are used at your home to separate mixtures. Also identify the time taken to separate particles from the mixtures.

Magnets

1. Fill in the blanks with the correct option.

a. Earth is a giant _____ magnet. (ring/bar)

b. Materials that are attracted by a magnet are called _____ substances. (manganese/magnetic)

c. The _____ poles of magnets attract each other. (unlike/like)

d. A magnet can lose its property when _____. (heated/used)

e. A _____ magnet looks like the English letter U. (horseshoe/ring)

2. Write T for true statements and F for false ones.

a. A magnet strongly attracts a glass jar. ☐

b. A magnet always points in East-West direction. ☐

c. Like poles of a magnet repel each other. ☐

d. A bar magnet is weaker than a ring magnet. ☐

e. Every magnet consists of two poles. ☐

3. Short answer questions.

a. Which type of material gets attracted by a magnet?
_____

b. What do you mean by the poles of a magnet?
_____

c. How many poles does a magnet have? Name them.
_____

d. Name two devices in which magnets are used.
_____

e. What is an artificial magnet?

4. Long answer questions.

a. How can we use a magnetic compass to find directions?

b. Explain the conditions in which two magnets attract or repel each other?

c. Why should we take care of the magnets?

d. Describe some important uses of magnets.

5. Think and write

Every magnet has two poles, North and South. Think about how you can identify the North and South poles of the given magnet. Explain how.

6. Activity time

Find out how you can make your own magnet. Try to make a magnet and check its strength by attracting different metallic objects with it.

Air and Water

1. **Fill in the blanks.**

    a. Salt is obtained from seawater by the process of _____.

    b. Clouds are a cluster of _____.

    c. Plants need _____ for photosynthesis.

    d. _____ gas supports burning.

    e. _____ is the cyclic movement of water.

2. **Write T for true statements and F for false ones.**

    a. Maximum water should be utilized for domestic purposes. ☐

    b. Water cycle involves only evaporation and condensation of water. ☐

    c. Plants use carbon dioxide and give out oxygen. ☐

    d. Water harvesting allows clouds to store more water. ☐

    e. Nitrogen is present in the maximum quantity in air. ☐

3. **Give two examples for the following.**

    a. Sources of salty water   _____, _____

    b. Causes of air pollution   _____, _____

    c. Gases in air   _____, _____

    d. Water pollutants   _____, _____

    e. Ways to save water   _____, _____

4. **Match the following.**

Column A	Column B
a. Freshwater source	Irrigation
b. Oxygen	3%
c. Artificial watering	78%
d. Nitrogen	Lake
e. Freshwater on Earth	21%

5. **Short answer questions.**

   a. Write three uses of water other than domestic purposes.

   b. What are some major components of air?

   c. How are clouds formed?

   d. What are some important sources of freshwater?

   e. How can a dam be helpful during floods or drought?

6. **Long answer questions.**

   a. How do plants help in maintaining the balance of oxygen and carbon dioxide in the air?

b. Explain water cycle and the processes it includes.

c. Write a short note on the importance of air to support life.

d. What is rainwater harvesting and how is it helpful to us?

e. Discuss the ways in which we can conserve water.

7. **Think and write**

   Air is also present in water which is used for breathing by fishes. Think and write the ways in which you can show the presence of air in water.

Waste Management

1. **Choose the correct option.**

   a. Wastes that can be decomposed

   ☐ Biodegradable ☐ Non-biodegradable

   b. It is a non-biodegradable waste

   ☐ Polythene bags ☐ Vegetable peels

   c. The product which should not be added to a vermicompost

   ☐ Animal products ☐ Dead leaves

   d. A component of the three R's

   ☐ Reduce ☐ Refuse

   e. It helps in the process of composting

   ☐ Bacteria ☐ Plastic

2. **Write T for true statements and F for false ones.**

   a. Old mobile phones can be decomposed. ☐

   b. Earthworms help in composting process. ☐

   c. Reducing waste is a better option than creating landfills. ☐

   d. Glass bottles take less time to decompose than paper. ☐

   e. Using both sides of paper helps to save trees. ☐

3. **Write whether the following are biodegradable or non-biodegradable.**

a. Plastic can _____

b. Left over fruits _____

c. Tissue paper _____

d. Used batteries _____

e. Dead plant parts _____

4. **Match the following.**

   Column A   **Column B**

   a. Kitchen waste   Reuse

   b. Plastic and glass waste   Vermicompost

   c. Red worms   Landfill

   d. Using bottles and jars again   Biodegradable

   e. Waste disposal land   Non-biodegradable

5. **Short answer question.**

a. Differentiate between biodegradable and non-biodegradable waste.
   _____

b. What is composting?
   _____

c. What are landfills? What is done when a landfill is full?
   _____

d. What are the ways to manage non-biodegradable waste efficiently?
   _____

e. How can we reduce the amount of waste?
_____

6. Long answer questions.

a. Explain the process of degradation.
_____
_____

b. Explain how a vermicompost works?
_____
_____

c. How is a landfill different from a vermicompost?
_____
_____

d. How is paper made? How can we save trees by recycling paper?
_____
_____

e. List some ways to reuse and recycle plastic.
_____
_____

7. Think and write

Some people burn dead leaves instead of making a compost. According to you, which one is a good practice? Justify your answer.
_____
_____
_____

8. Activity time

Make a colourful poster on the topic "Green City, Clean City." Also add a suitable slogan to it.

Light and Reflection

1. **Fill in the blanks using the correct option.**

   a. Reflection from a rough surface is called _____ reflection. (diffused/infused)

   b. A _____ does not undergo lateral inversion. (image/shadow)

   c. The _____ of the shadow can vary. (colour/size)

   d. A group of light rays moving together is called a _____. (beam/bumps)

   e. A shadow can only show the _____ of an object. (size/shape)

2. **Give two examples of the following:**

   a. Luminous objects   _____, _____

   b. Non-luminous objects   _____, _____

   c. Smooth surface   _____, _____

   d. Rough surface   _____, _____

   e. Opaque materials   _____, _____

3. **Short answer questions.**

   a. On what basis do we classify objects as transparent and opaque?

   _____

   b. How is a shadow formed?

   _____

c. Which type of material cannot have a shadow?
_____

d. Define the process of propagation.
_____

e. What do you mean by reflection of light?
_____

f. Why is it advised to use a smooth surface for making mirrors?
_____

4. Answer the following questions.

a. What is a ray? What are the two types of beam?
_____
_____

b. Explain the characteristics of a shadow.
_____
_____

c. What is lateral reflection? How does it take place?
_____
_____

d. How is the image of an object different from its shadow?
_____
_____

e. With the help of a diagram, represent how a pinhole camera works.

_____
_____

5. Think and write

Suppose you are walking on the street outside your house in the evening and you can see multiple shadows of a stray dog. Is it possible to have multiple shadows? Explain your answer with constructive comments.

_____
_____
_____
_____

6. Activity time

Take objects of different sizes and form their shadows. Try to make the shadow of the smaller object larger than the shadow of the bigger object. Examine the various factors which change the shadow of an object.

Electricity

1. Fill in the blanks.

a. The _____ of a bulb heats up to give us light.

b. A collection of cells is called a _____.

c. Electric current flows only if the circuit is _____.

d. A switch is sometimes referred to as _____.

e. An insulator is a _____ conductor of electricity.

2. Give two examples of the following:

a. Source of electric current _____, _____

b. Electric cells _____, _____

c. Conductors _____, _____

d. Insulators _____, _____

e. Electrical devices _____, _____

3. Define the following terms.

a. Dry Cell _____

b. Battery _____

c. Electric circuit _____

d. Conductor _____

e. Insulator _____

4. **Answer the following questions.**

a. What is an electrical switch? Name two devices with such a switch.

b. List the three conditions for an electric current to flow.

c. Explain the two types of electric cells with examples of each.

d. How can we check whether a given material is a conductor or an insulator?

e. Why should we keep ourselves safe from electricity?

f. Draw a labelled circuit diagram to show the working of an electric bulb.

5. Think and write

Electricity is very useful to us but it can also be dangerous. Comment on the statement taking examples from your daily life.

_____
_____
_____
_____

6. Activity time

Use the library resources and find about the invention of electric cell. Also find out the stories of invention of other electric devices such as bulb, fan, computers etc.

Answers

Biotic and Abiotic
1. a. producers   b. cold-blooded
   c. water   d. carbon dioxide
   e. response
2. a. F   b. T   c. F
   d. F   e. T
3. a. Autotrophs   b. Detritivores
   c. Topsoil   d. Cell
   e. Temperature
5. a. Amoeba   b. Plants
   c. Fungi   d. Vulture
   e. Water

Features of Plants
1. a. Parallel   b. petals
   c. roots   d. longer
   e. water
2. a. T   b. F   c. F
   d. T   e. T
3. a. Banana, Grapes   b. Apple, Papaya
   c. Potato, Ginger   d. Onion, Garlic
   e. Mangroves, Radish   f. Carrot, Beetroot
   g. Maize, Rice
4. a. Modified stem   b. Modified stem
   c. Modified leaves   d. Parallel venation
   e. Reticulate venation

Animal Movements
1. a. hinge   b. streamlined
   c. exoskeleton   d. marrow
   e. Cartilage
2. a. Snail, Snake   b. Donkey, Pig
   c. Turtle, Fish   d. Hen, Peacock
   e. Monkey, Spider
3. a. strong   b. outer
   c. flexible   d. movable
   e. with

Adapting to Habitat
1. a. grasslands   b. yak
   c. aquatic   d. blowholes
   e. Deciduous
2. a. F   b. T   c. F   d. F   e. T
4. a. Octopus, Coral   b. Duck, Water Lily
   c. Woodpecker, Oak   d. Beaver, Pine
   e. Sloth, Rubber tree   f. Elephant, Buffalo Grass
   g. Camel, Prickly Pear   h. Bear, Cedar
   i. Polar Bear, Mosses

Components of Food
1. a. energy   b. trace nutrients
   c. starch and sugar   d. Vitamin B 12
   e. Unsaturated
2. a. F   b. T   c. T   d. F
   e. F
3. a. Iodine   b. Vitamin D
   c. Calcium   d. Vitamin B
   e. Vitamin C   f. Iron
   g. Vitamin A
4. a. Milk, Meat   b. Oil, Nuts
   c. Corn, Potato   d. Honey, Fruits
   e. Figs, Carrots

Fibre to Fabric
1. a. fabric   b. plant
   c. yarn   d. knitting
   e. Polyester
2. a. F   b. T   c. F
   d. T   e. F
3. a. Rope, Sack   b. Shirt, Towel
   c. Parachute, Dress   d. Shoes, Paper
   e. Linen, Flaxseed oil
4. a. Kapok   b. Jute
   c. Coir   d. Cotton
   e. Flax

Classifying Materials
1. a. Solids   b. opaque
   c. insulated   d. Metals
   e. gas
2. a. F   b. T   c. F
   d. F   e. T
3. a. No, Yes, No, No   b. No, No, No, No
   c. Yes, No, Yes, Yes   d. No, No, No, No
   e. No, Yes, No, No
4. a. Rock, Bark of tree
   b. Flower petals, Feather
   c. Coloured glass, oiled paper
   d. Clean water, Glass
   e. Gold, Silver

Separation of Substances
1. a. F   b. T   c. F
   d. T   e. F
2. a. Irreversible   b. Irreversible
   c. Reversible   d. Reversible
   e. Reversible
3. a. Chemical   b. Physical

c. Chemical   d. Physical
e. Chemical

Changes Around Us
1. a. Direction of wind   b. Husk
   c. Sedimentation   d. Hand-picking
   e. Hits a cool surface
2. a. T   b. F   c. F
   d. T   e. F
4. a. Water   b. Sugar
   c. Chocolate   d. Carbon dioxide
   e. Humidity

Magnets
1. a. bar   b. magnetic
   c. unlike   d. heated
   e. horseshoe
2. a. F   b. F   c. T
   d. F   e. T

Air and Water
1. a. Evaporation   b. tiny water droplets
   c. air and water   d. Oxygen
   e. water cycle
2. a. F   b. F   c. T
   d. F   e. T
3. a. Ocean, Sea
   b. Automobiles, Factories
   c. Nitrogen, Oxygen
   d. Garbage, Chemicals
   e. Rainwater harvesting, Dams
4. a. Lake   b. 21%   c. Irrigation
   d. 78%   e. 3%

Waste Management
1. a. Biodegradable   b. Polythene bags
   c. Animal products   d. Reduce
   e. Bacteria
2. a. F   b. T   c. T
   d. F   e. T
3. a. Non - biodegradable
   b. Biodegradable
   c. Biodegradable
   d. Non - biodegradable
   e. Biodegradable
4. a. Biodegradable
   b. Non - biodegradable
   c. Vermicompost
   d. Reuse
   e. Landfill

Light and Reflection
1. a. diffused   b. shadow
   c. size   d. beam
   e. shape
2. a. Sun, Lamp   b. Wood, Wall
   c. Mirror, Glass   d. Brick wall, Rough paper
   e. Book, Cloth

Electricity
1. a. filament   b. battery
   c. closed   d. key
   e. bad
2. a. Cell, Battery
   b. Dry cells, Secondary Battery
   c. Rubber, Wood
   d. Iron, Aluminium
   e. Microwave Oven, Refrigerator

Made in the USA
Monee, IL
03 May 2026

49438753R00028